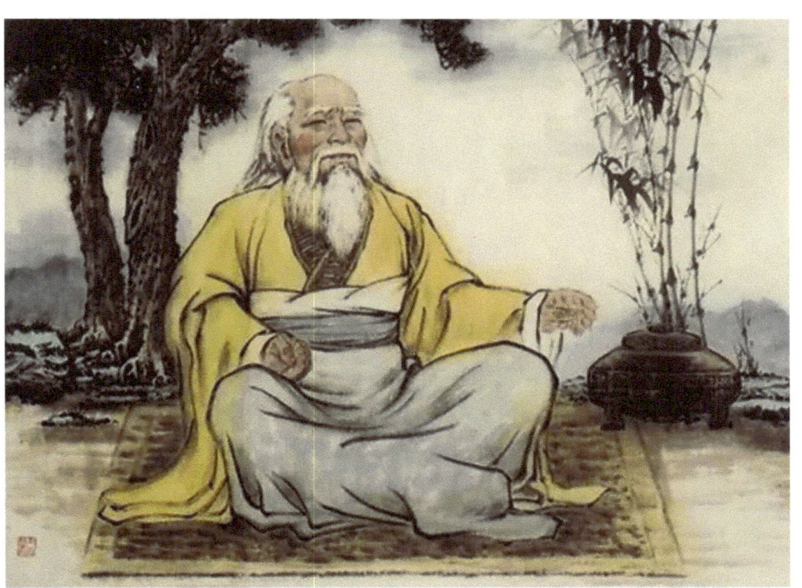

Lao Tzu

Without travel
one can know the
whole world.

Without looking out
of the window
one can see the Way.

The further one goes
the less one knows.

Turn the page to open the door

You are the window
through which
you must see the world

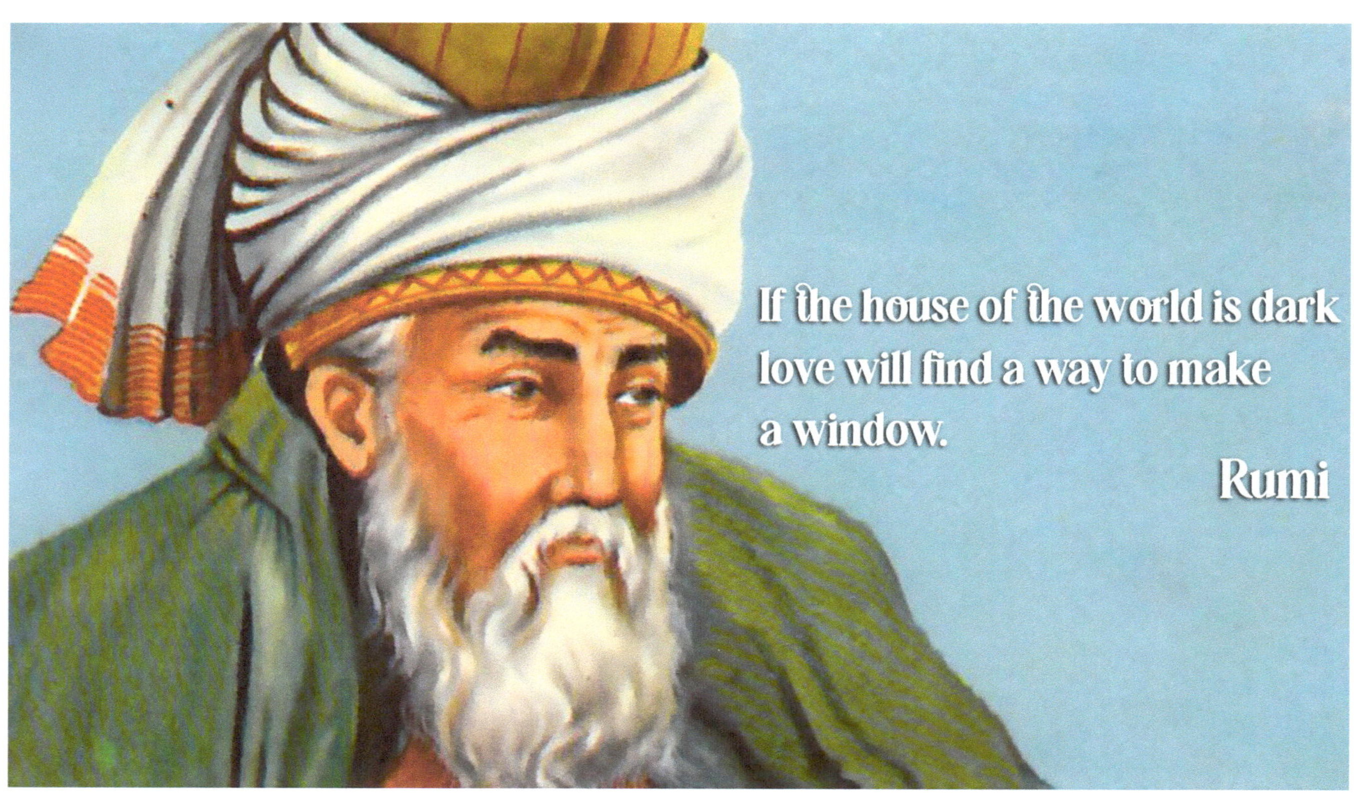
If the house of the world is dark
love will find a way to make
a window.
Rumi

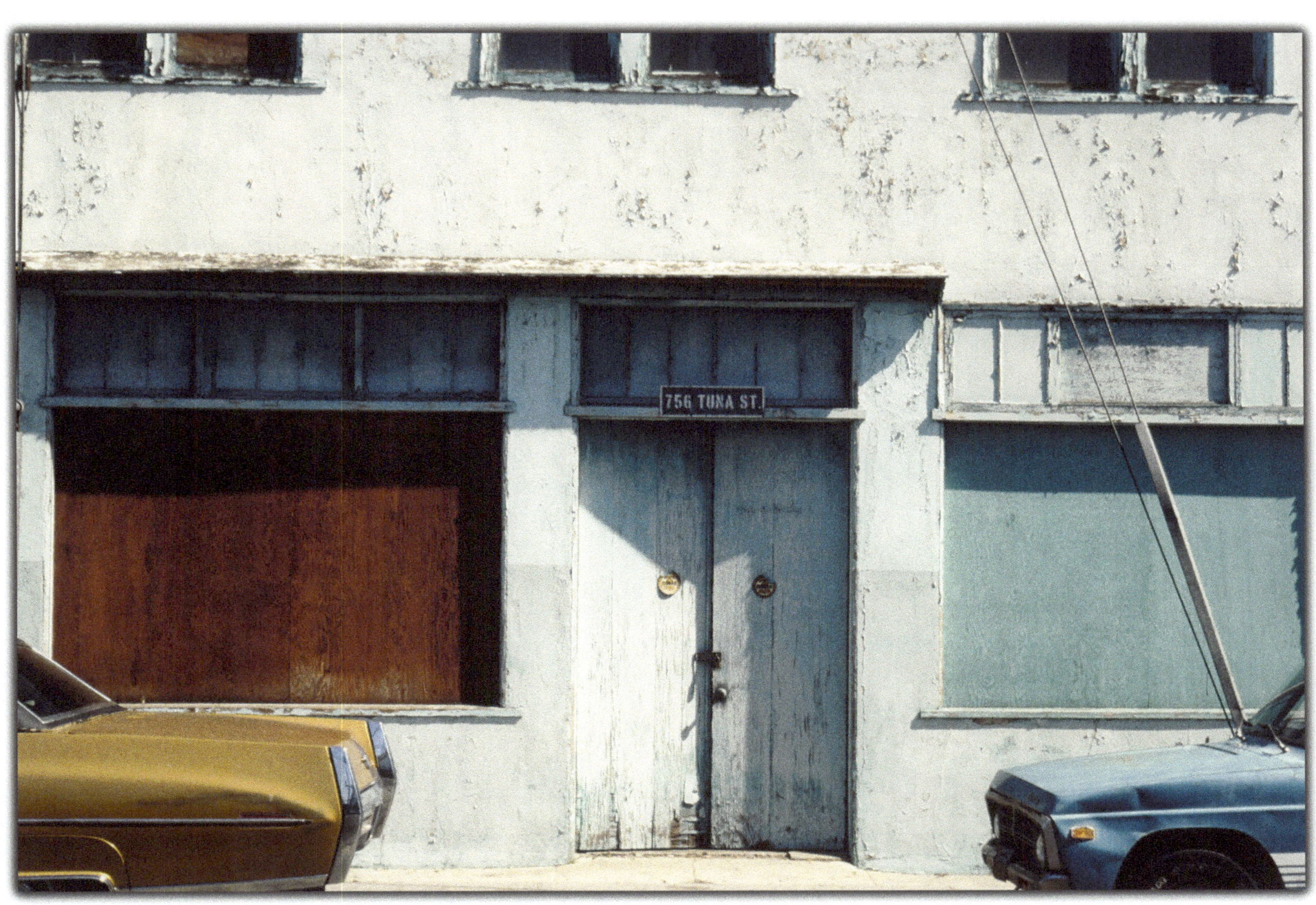
756 TUNA ST.

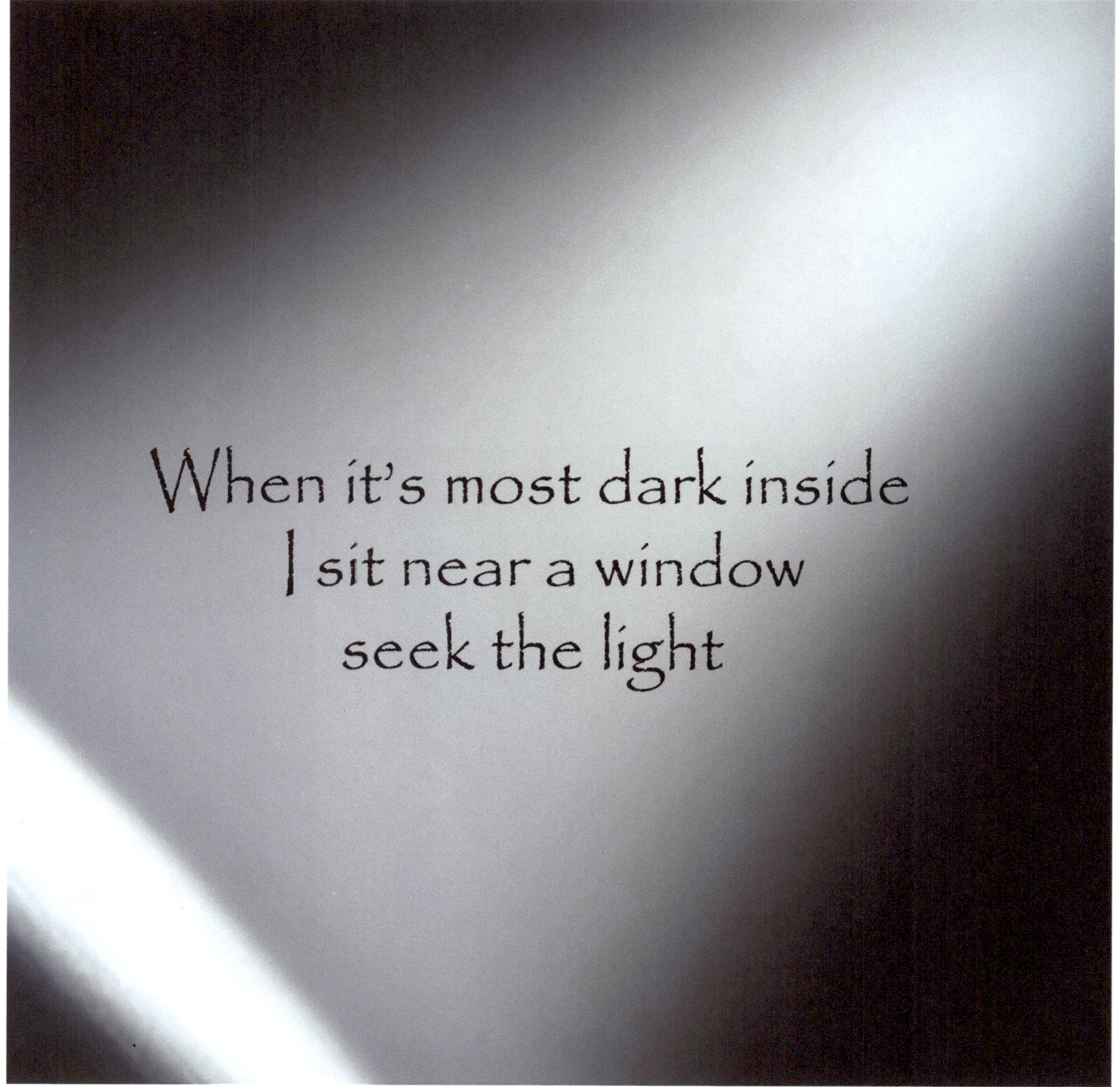
When it's most dark inside
I sit near a window
seek the light

The paradox of light & dark
is that neither can exist
without the other.

As hard as it may try
a window cannot keep them apart.

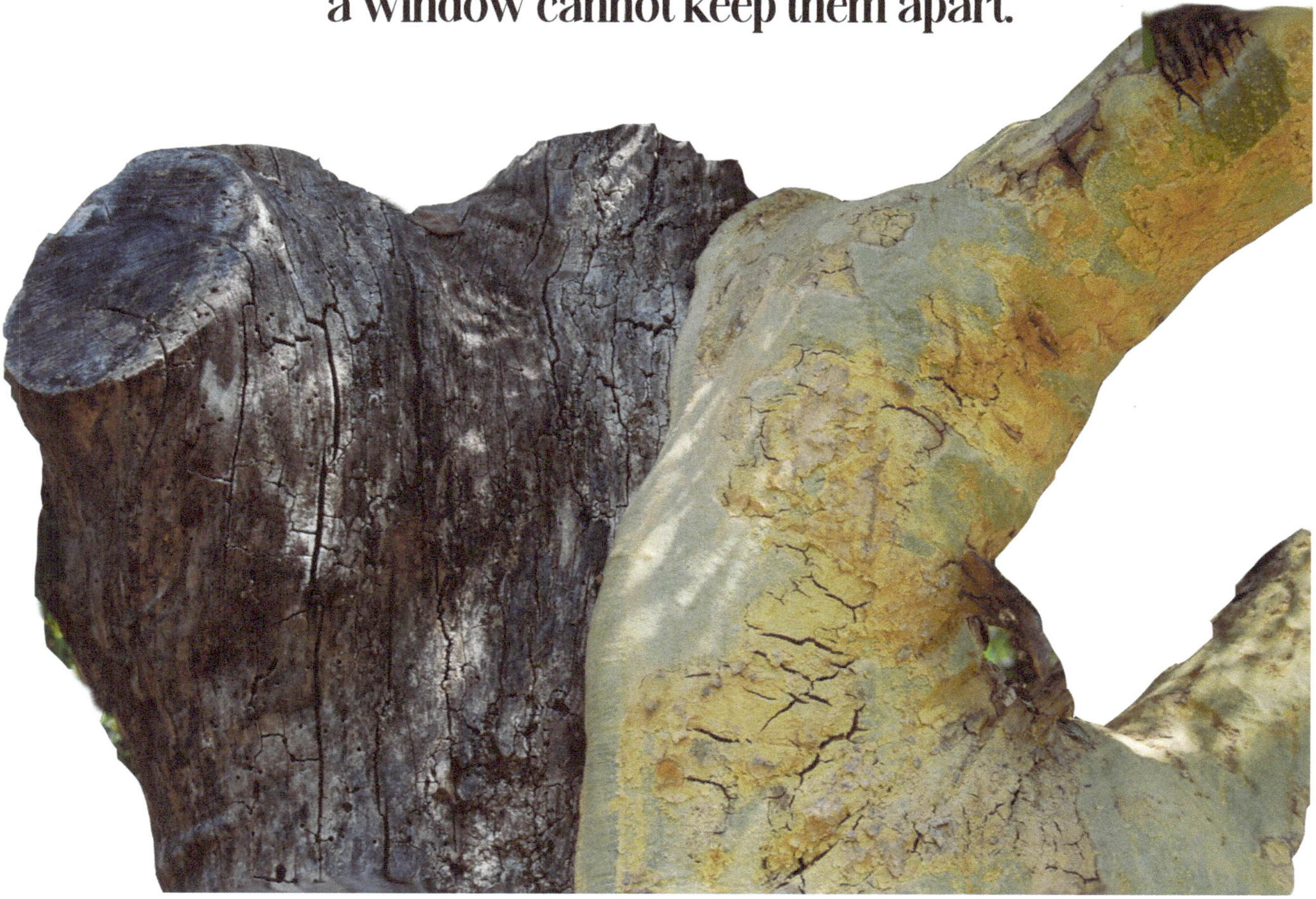

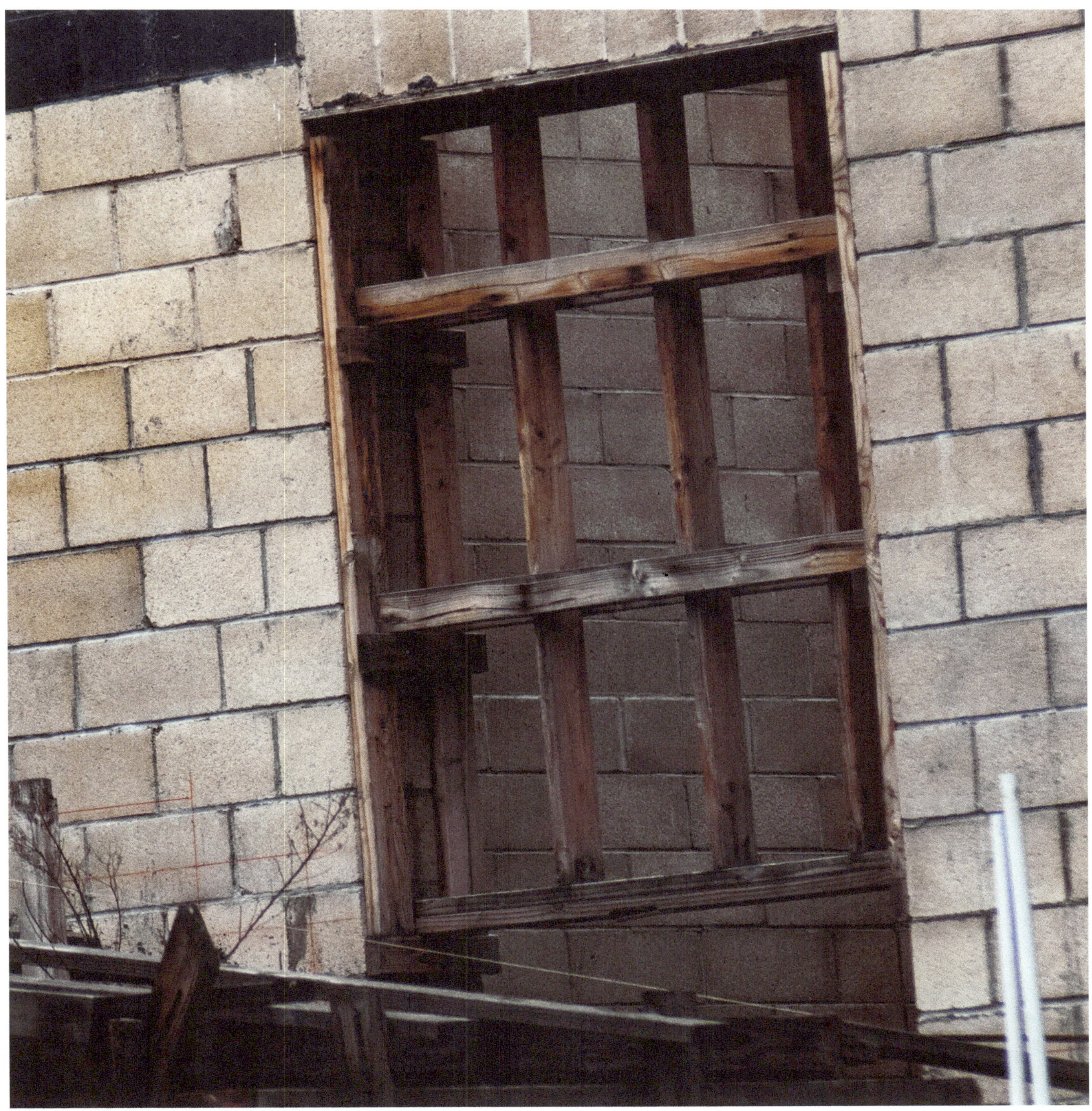

Janus, the Roman god of Doors
looks both ways..

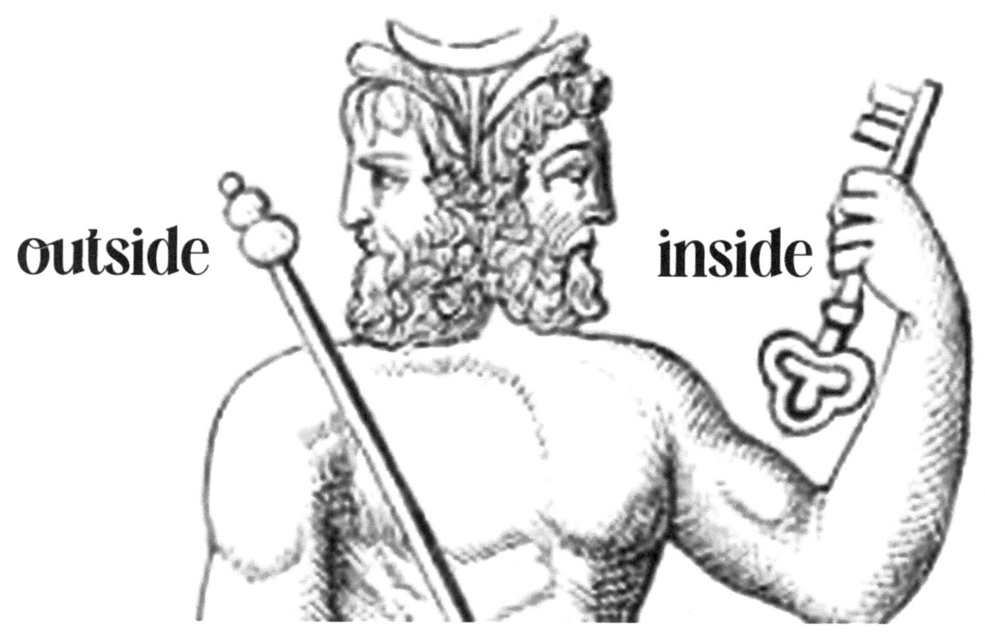

Through his eyes
we see the possible
& the lost.

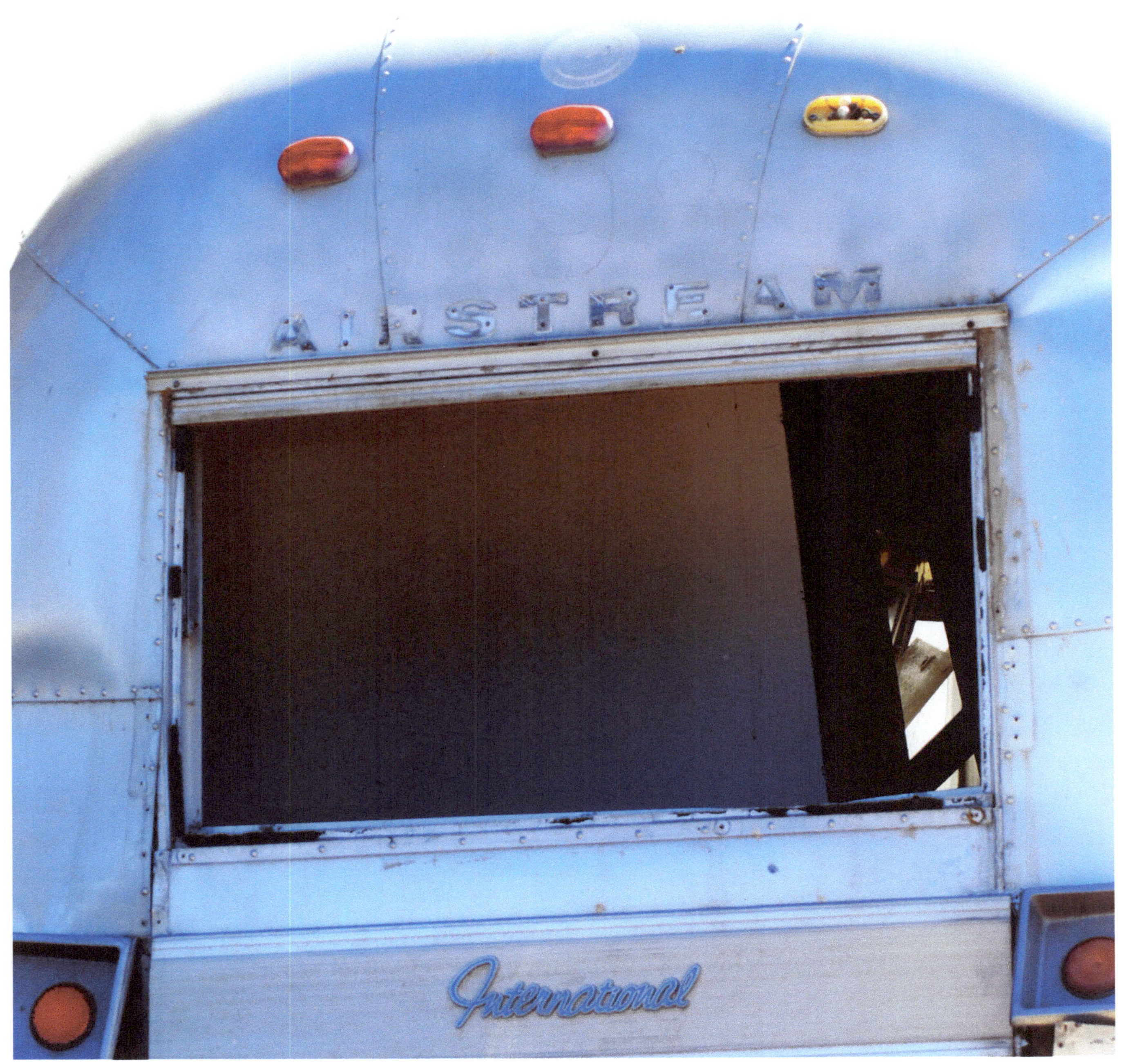
AIRSTREAM
International

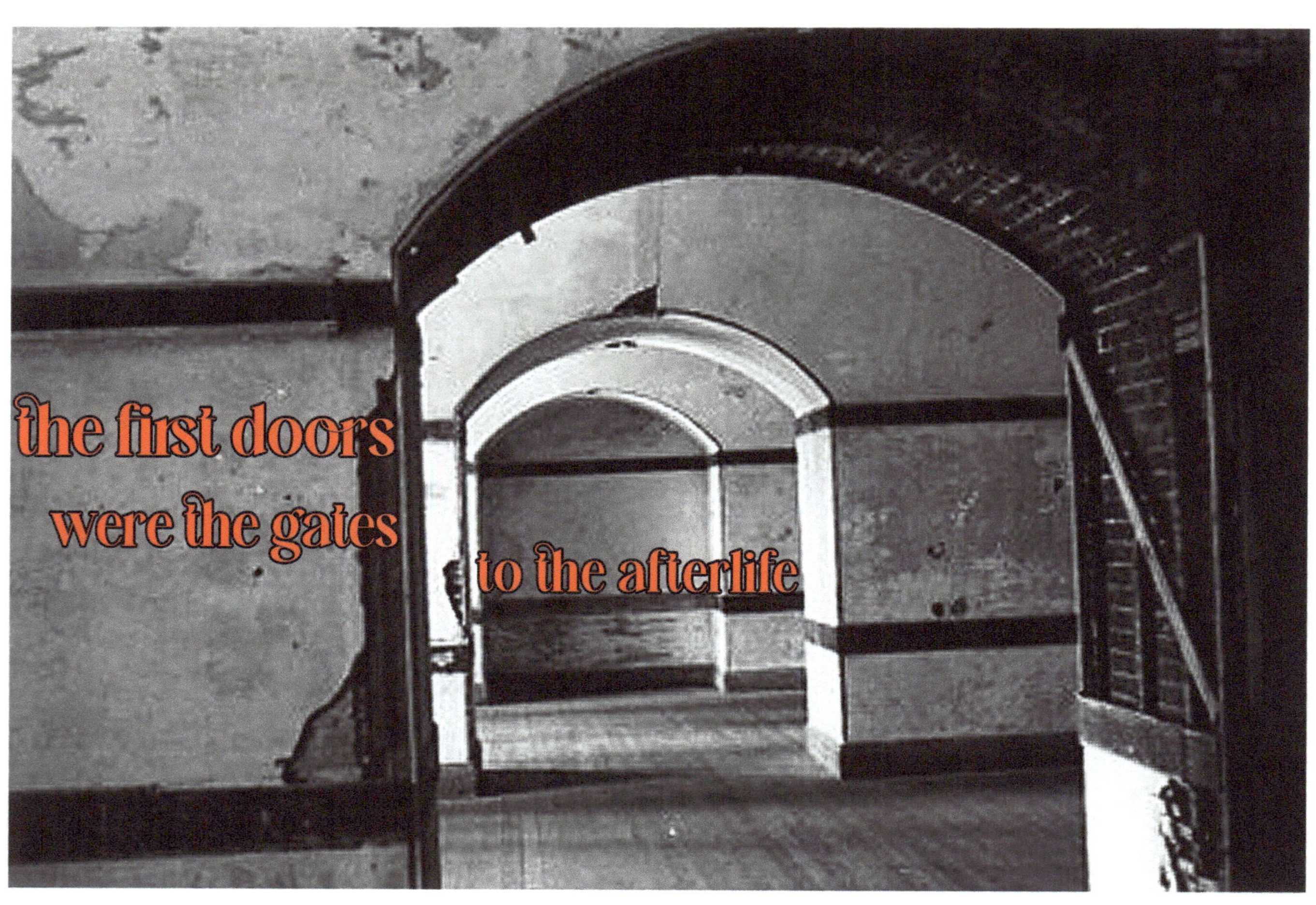
the first doors
were the gates
to the afterlife

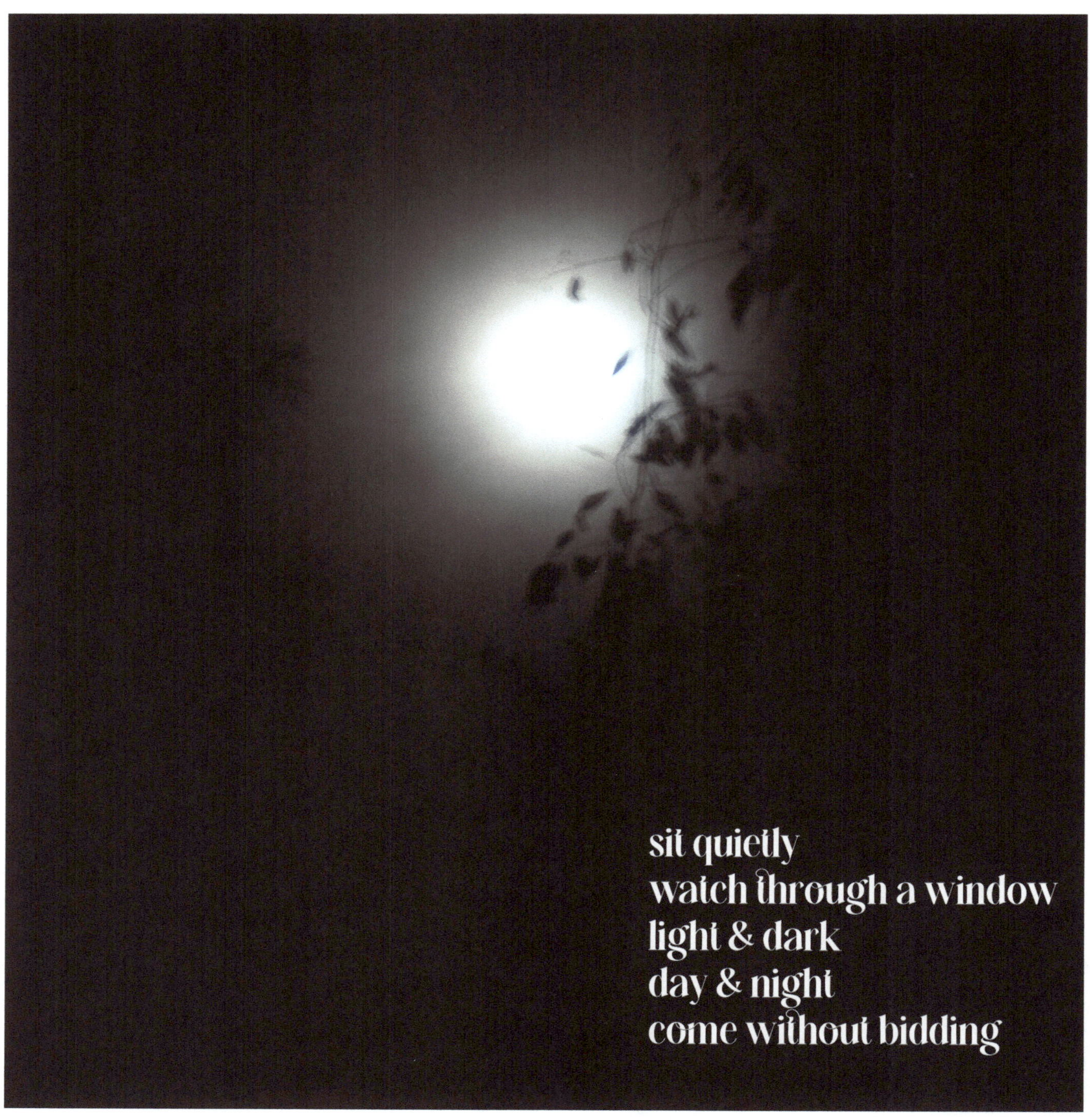
sit quietly
watch through a window
light & dark
day & night
come without bidding

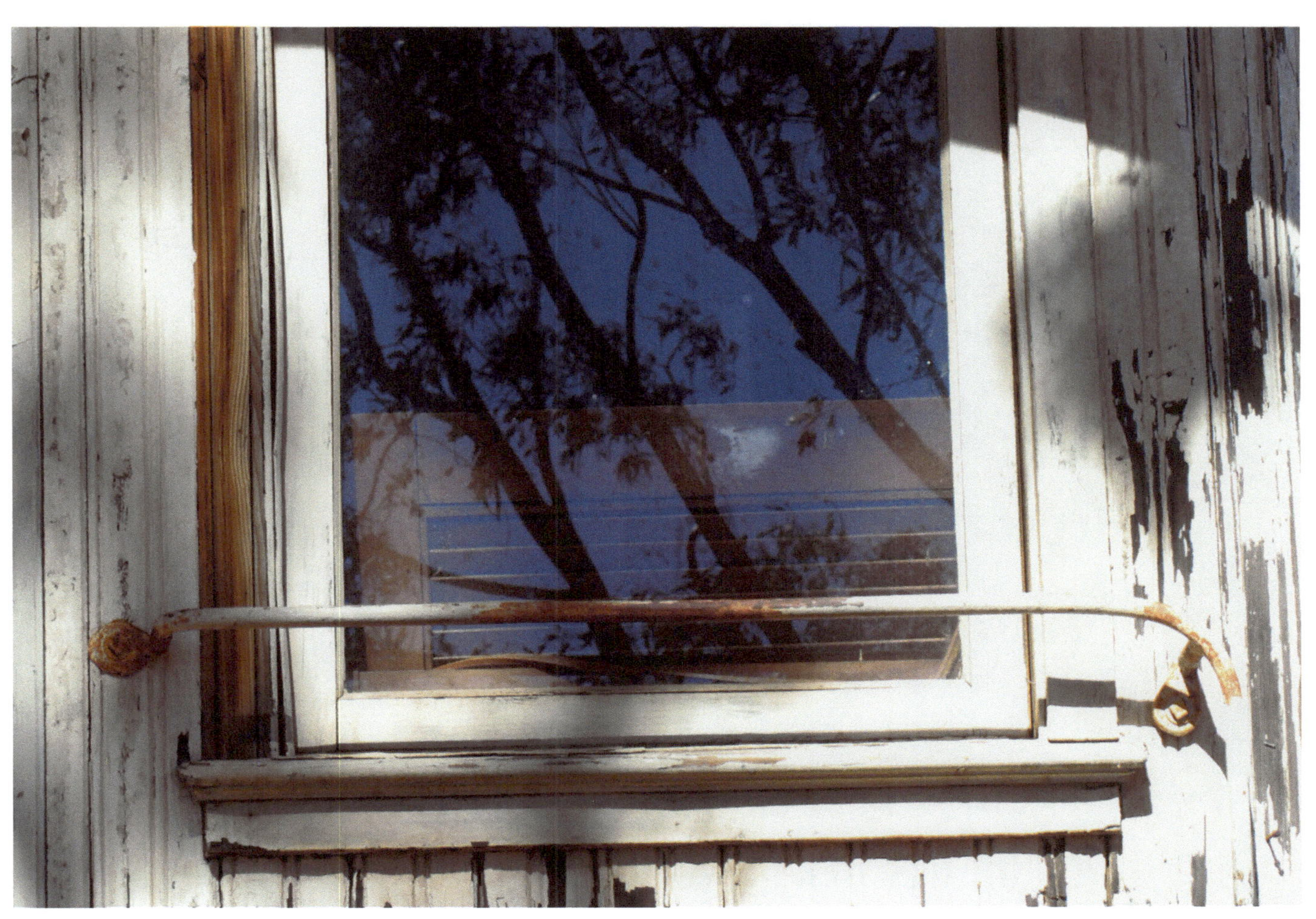

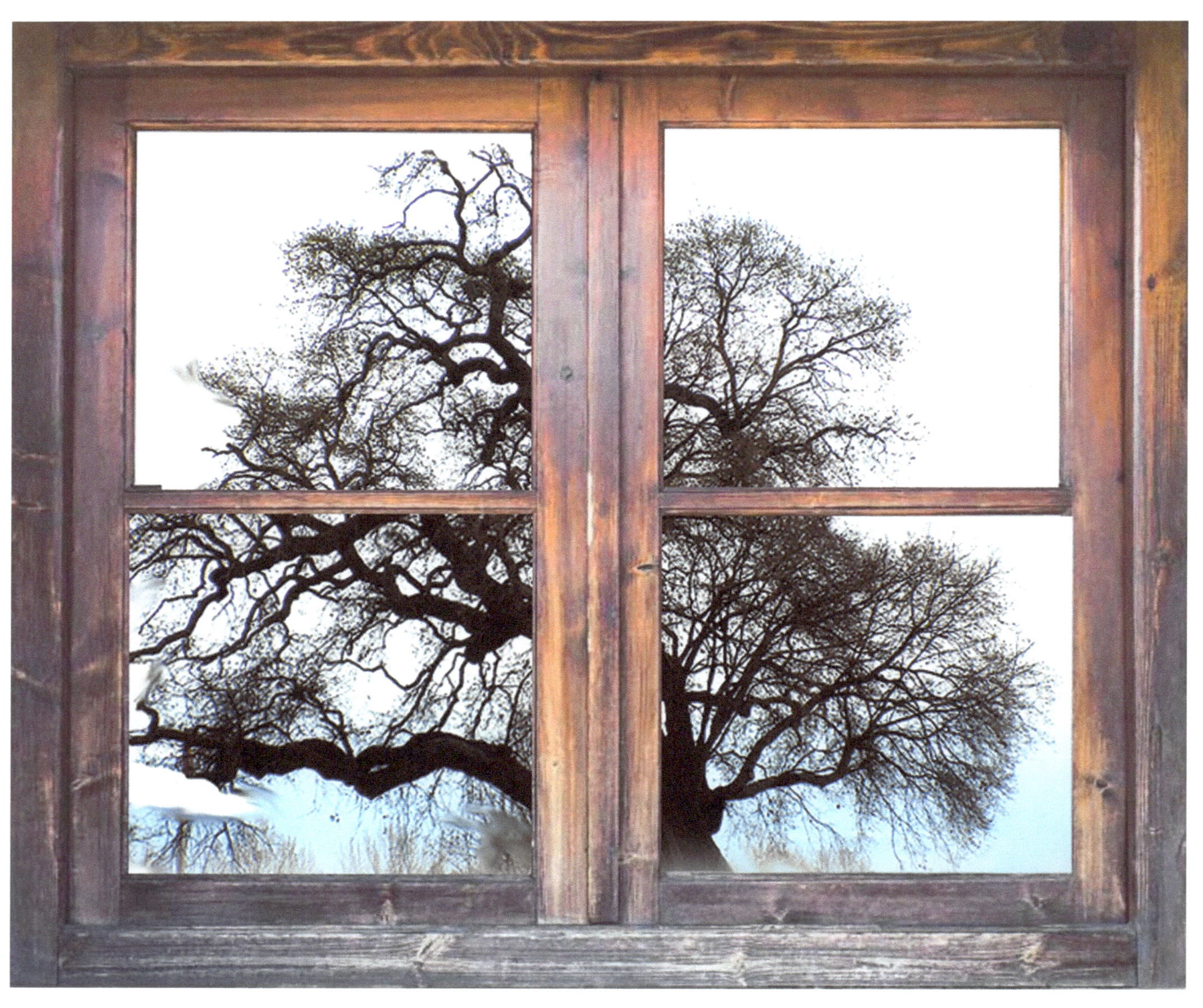

the tree that grows outside my window
has planted roots deep into my heart

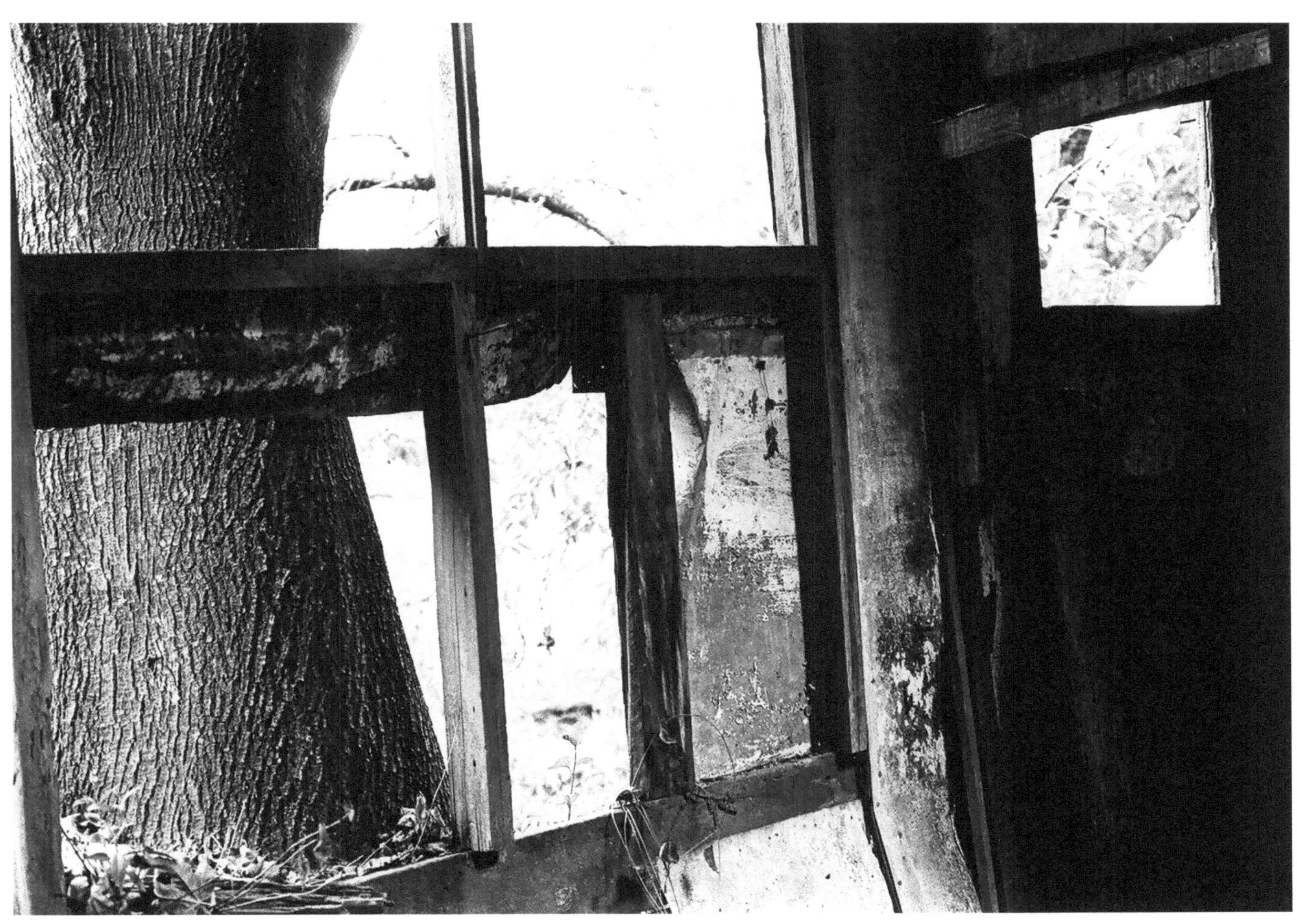

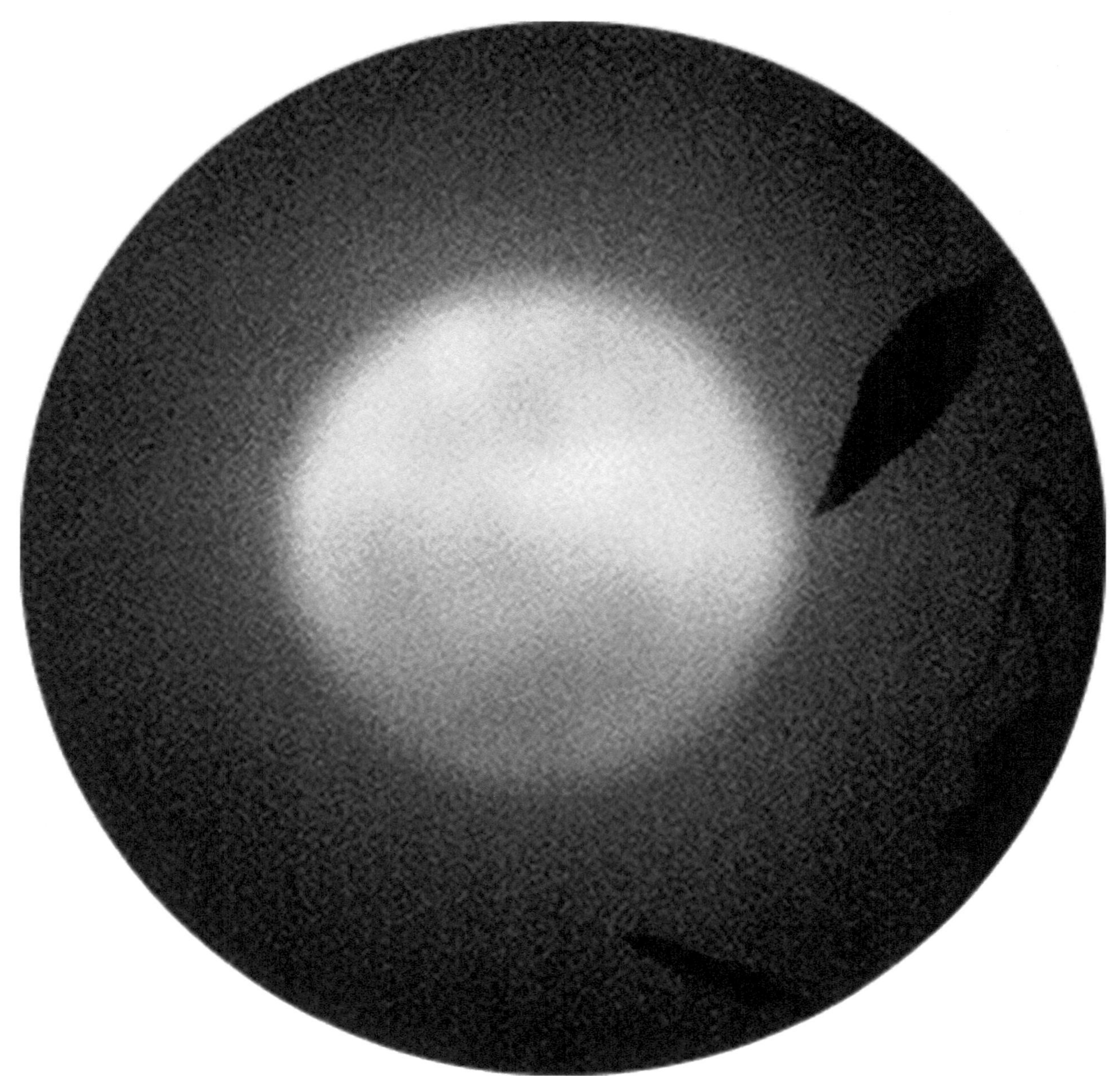

I dream it's only a closed window
that keeps me from holding the moon

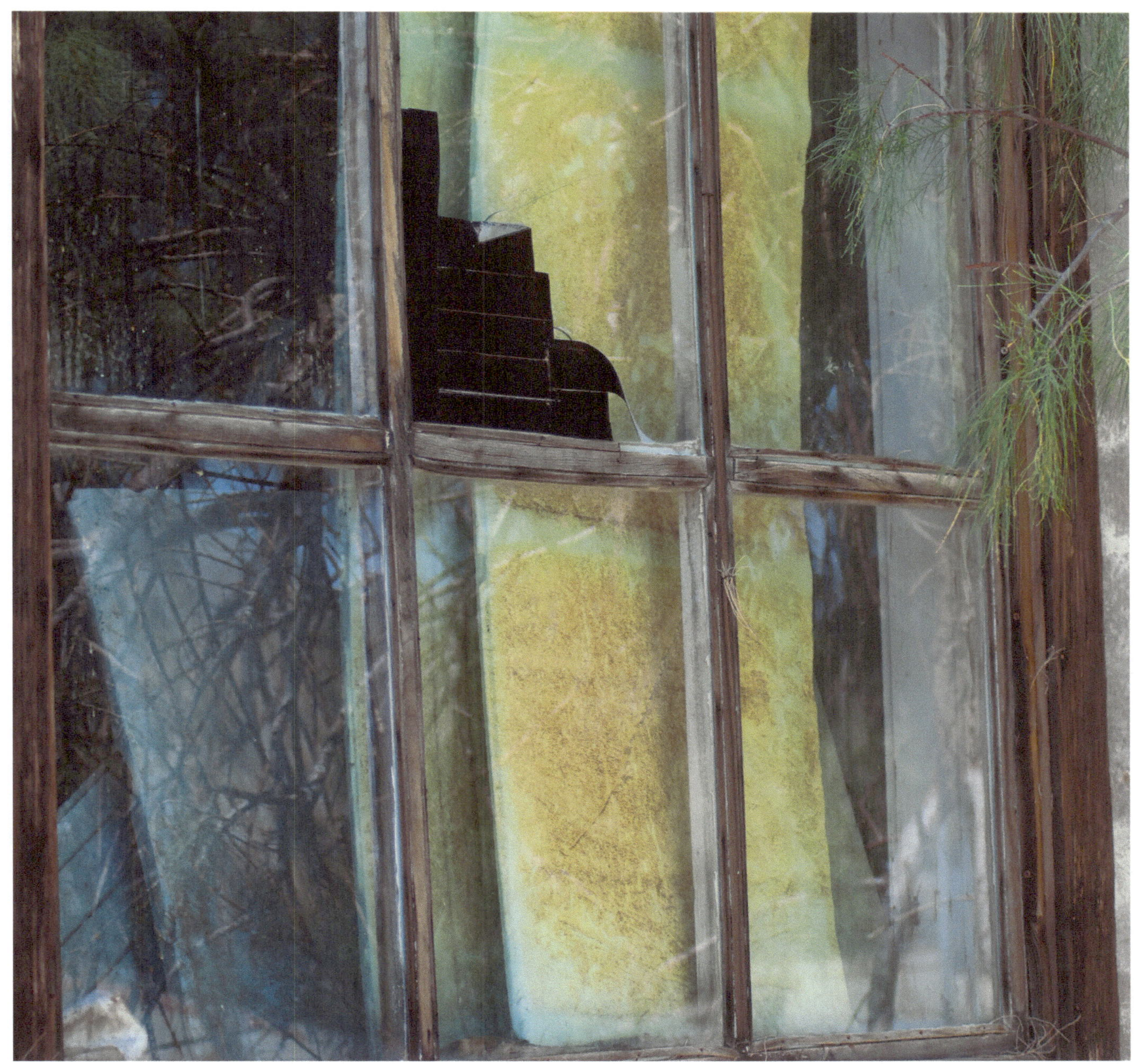

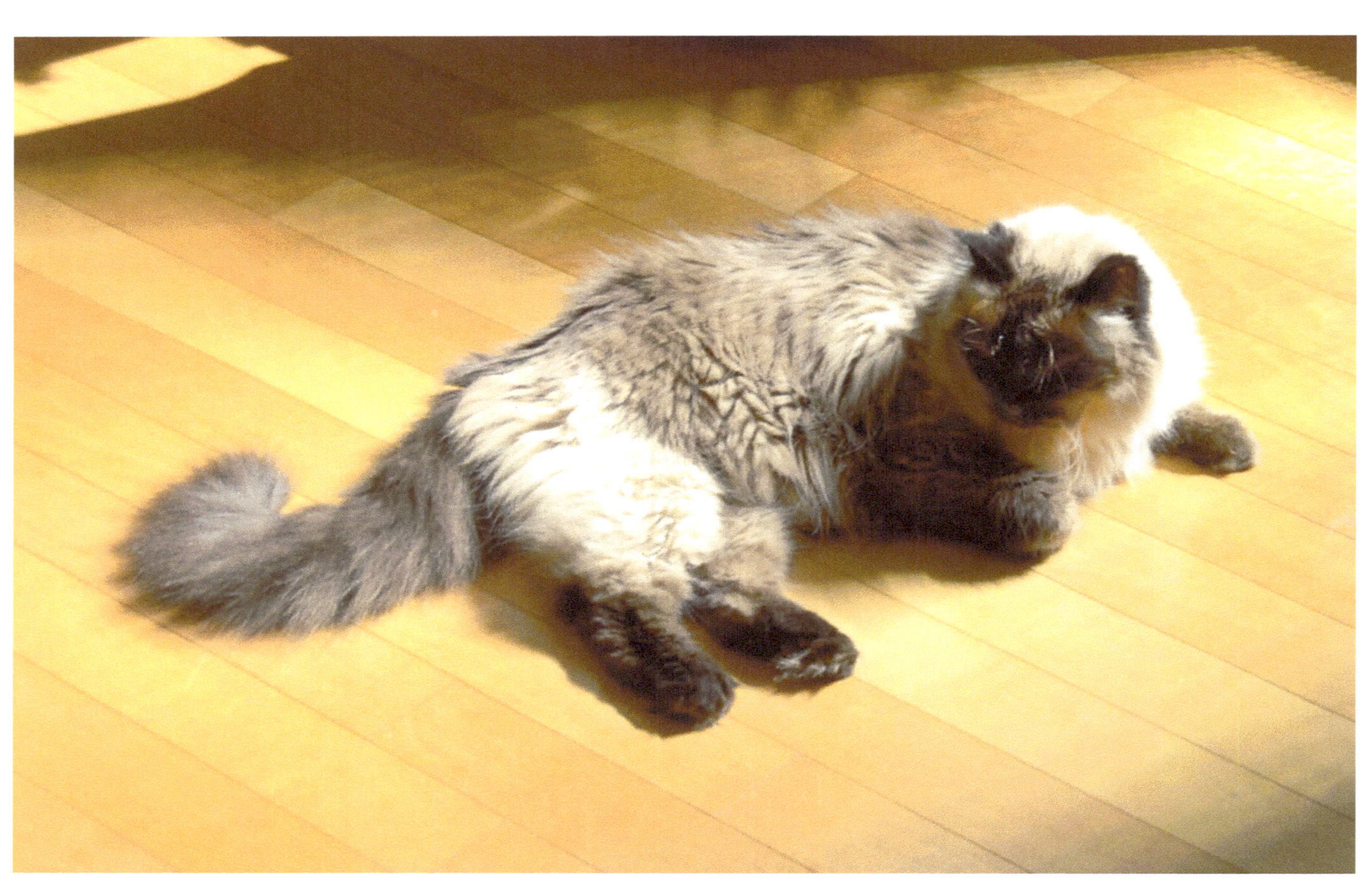

even in the darkest room
there is the chance of light
through the window

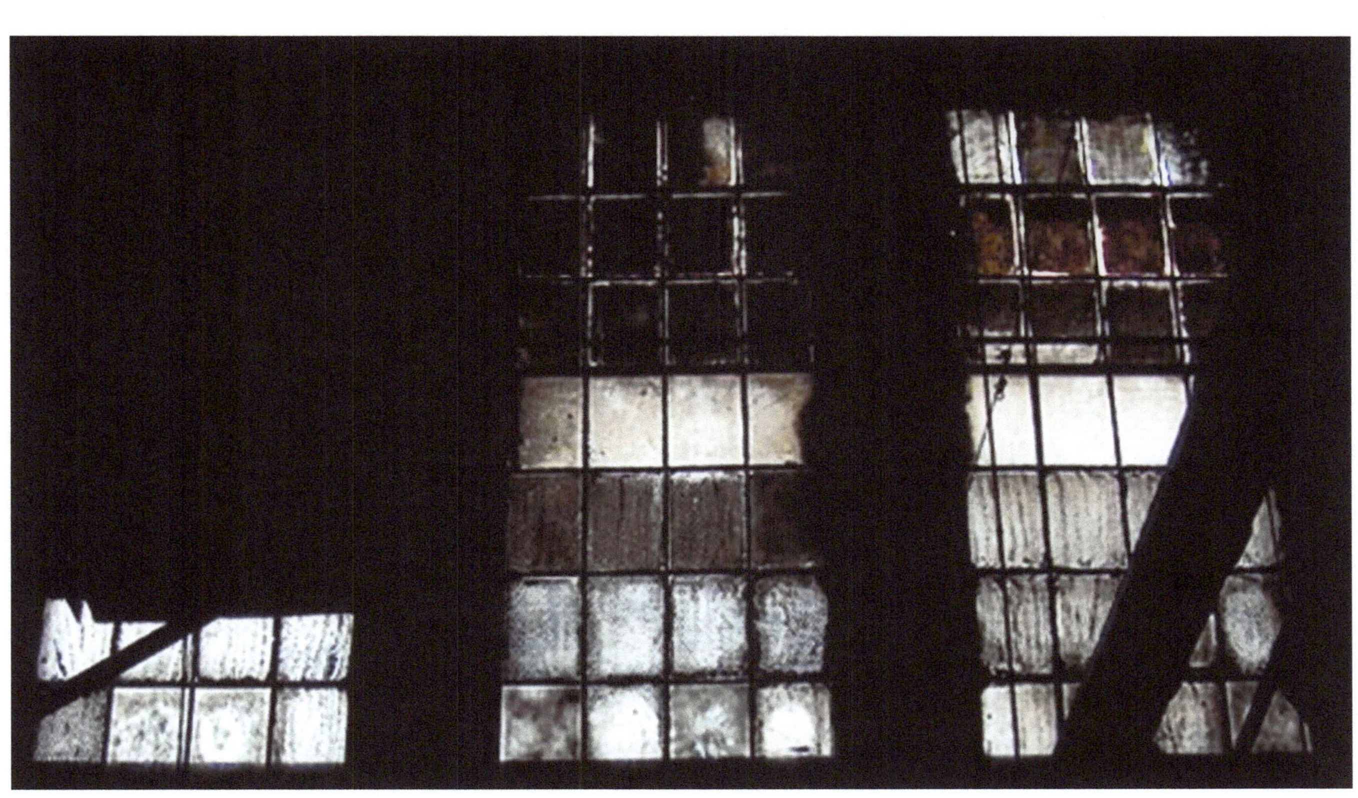

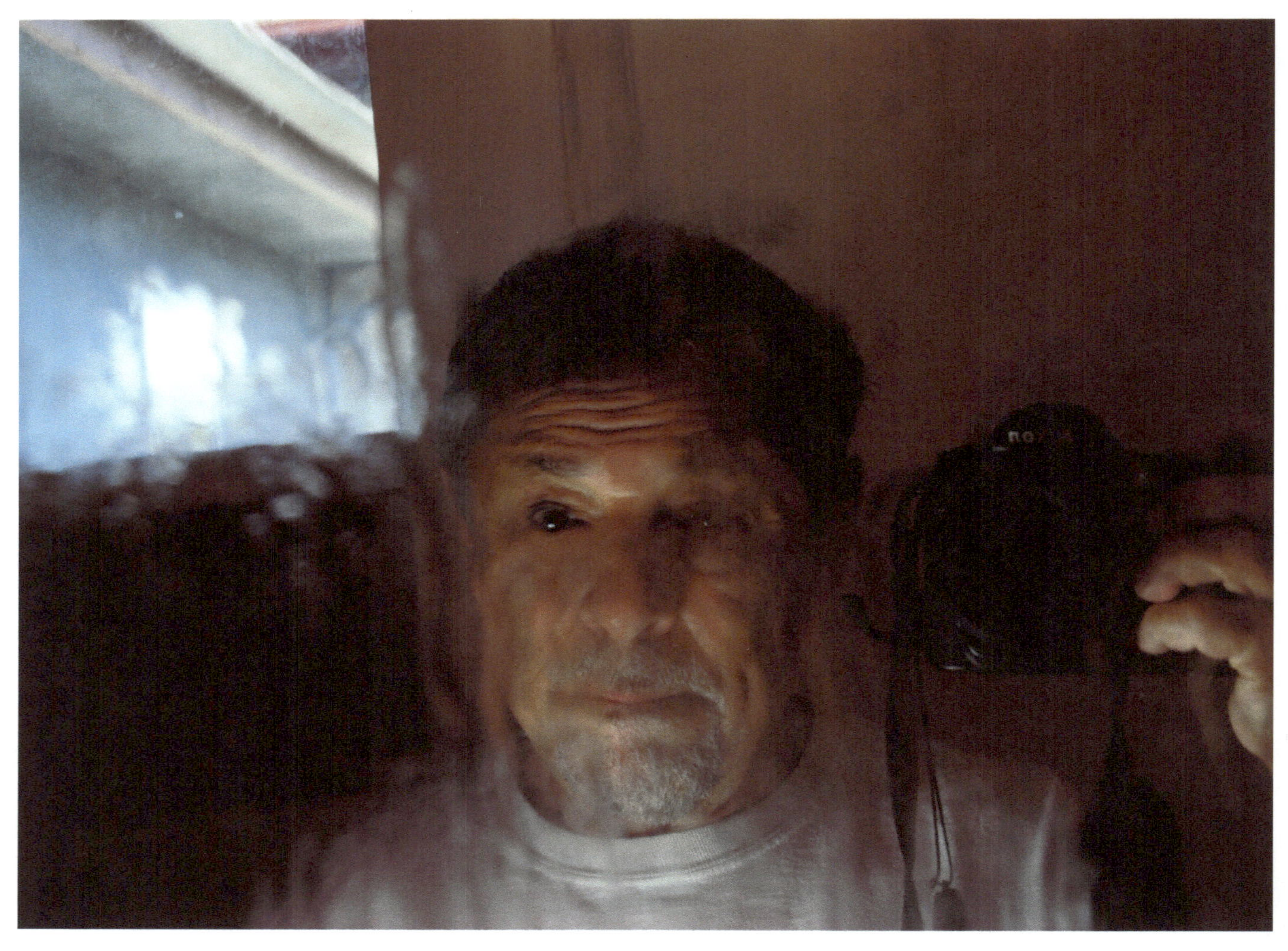

is there anything sadder
than rain streaking a window
reminding one of
the last time they cried

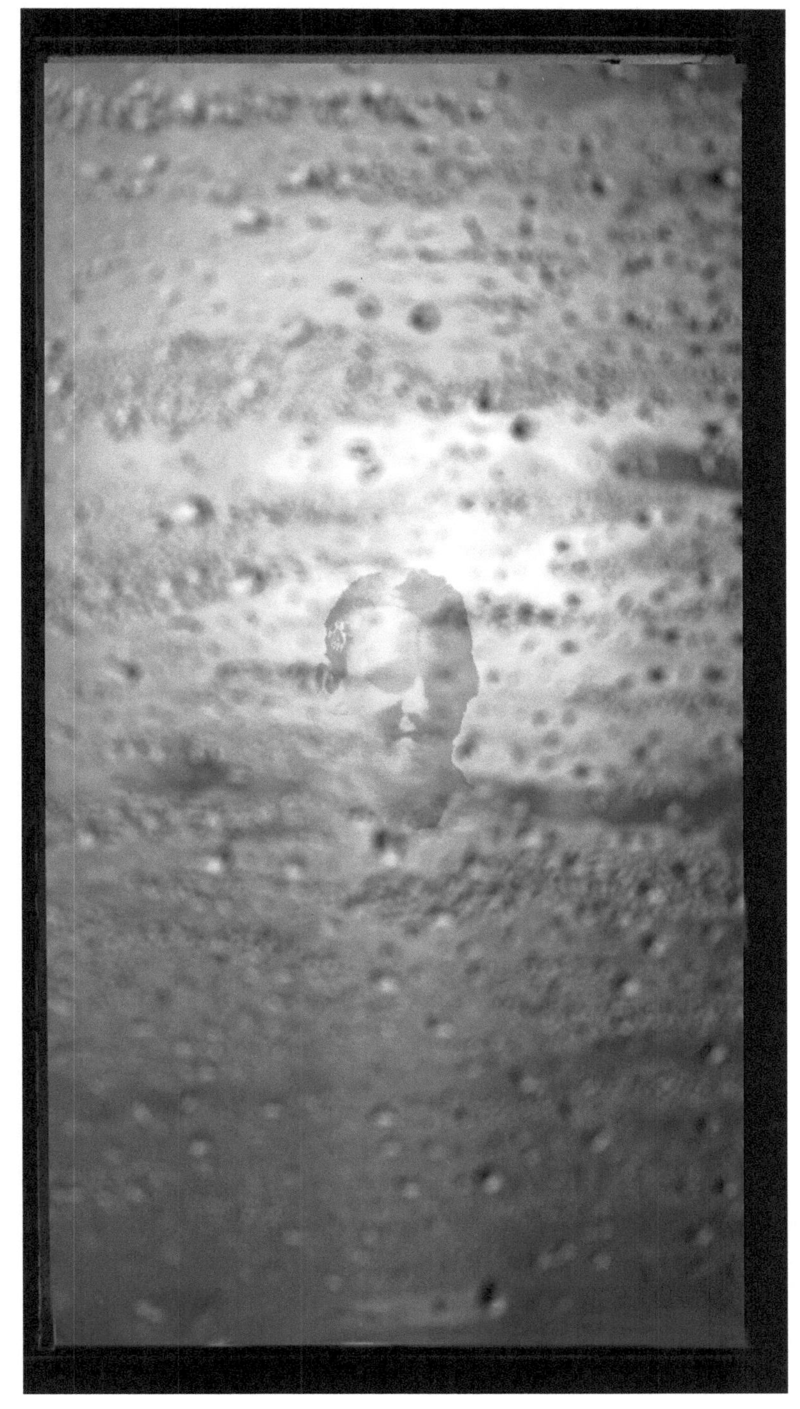

if I see light
ahead
feel
darkness
behind
do I cherish
the light
or turn
& embrace
the dark

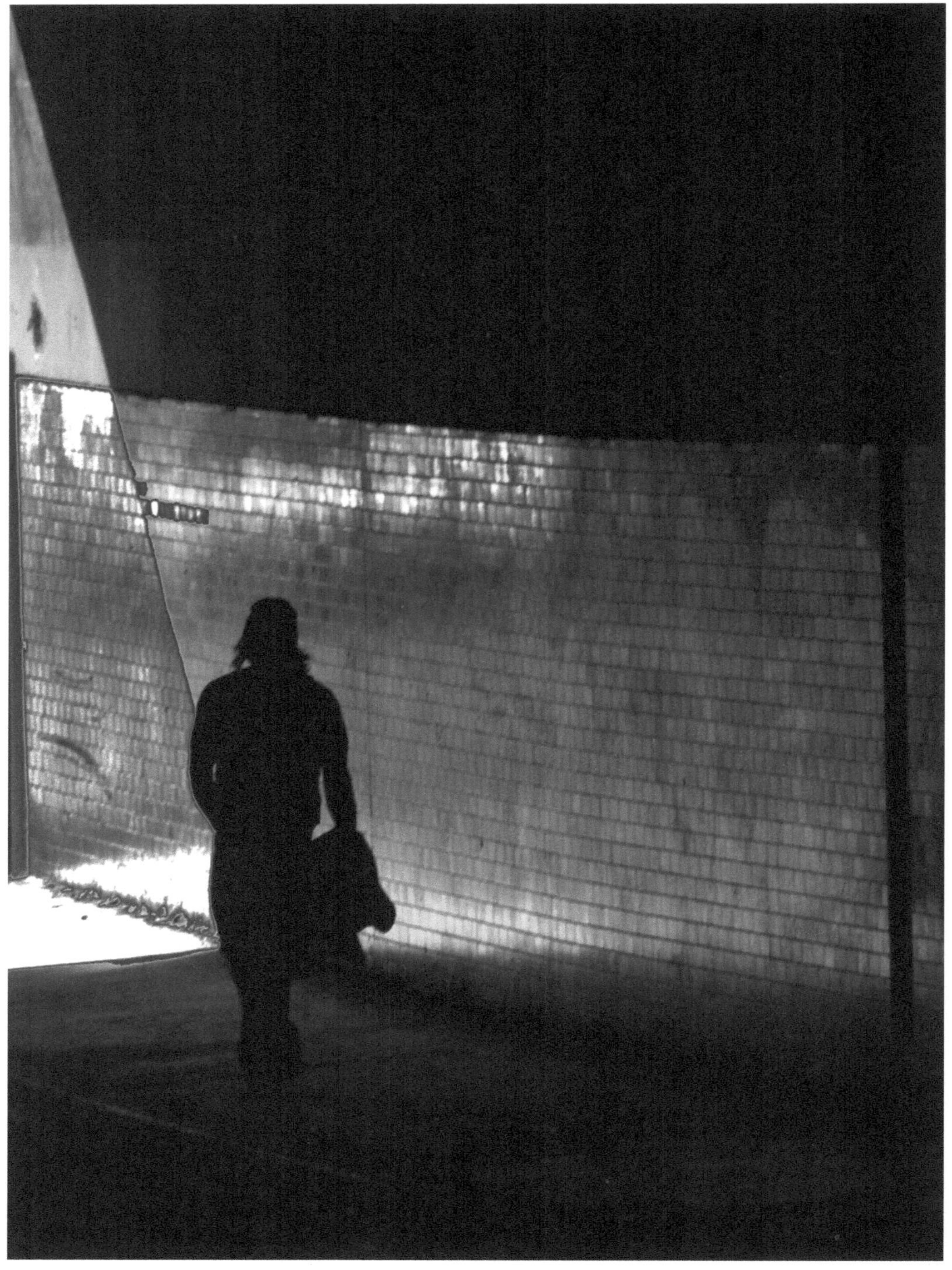

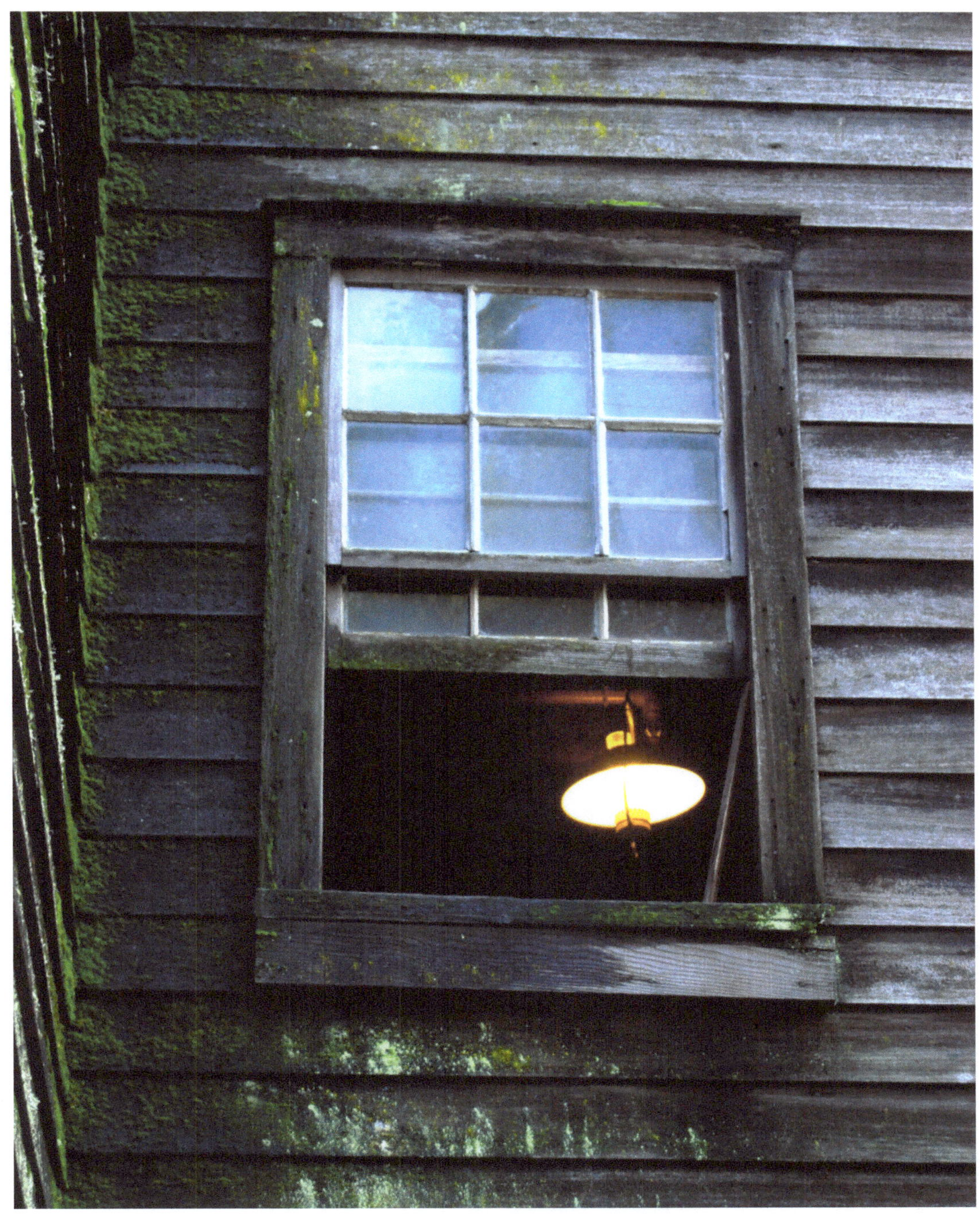

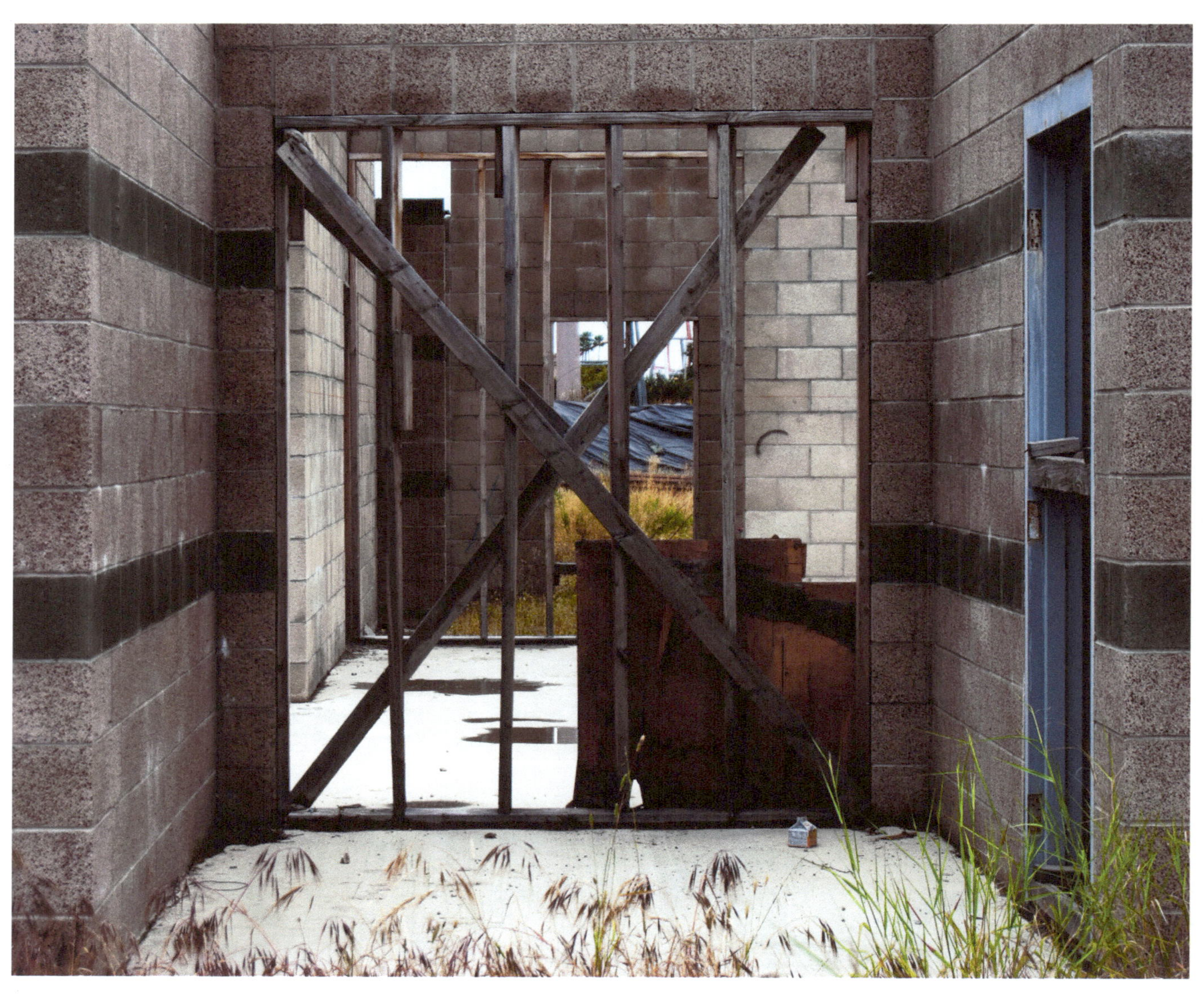

Inside or outside -
depends upon which side of the door you're standing

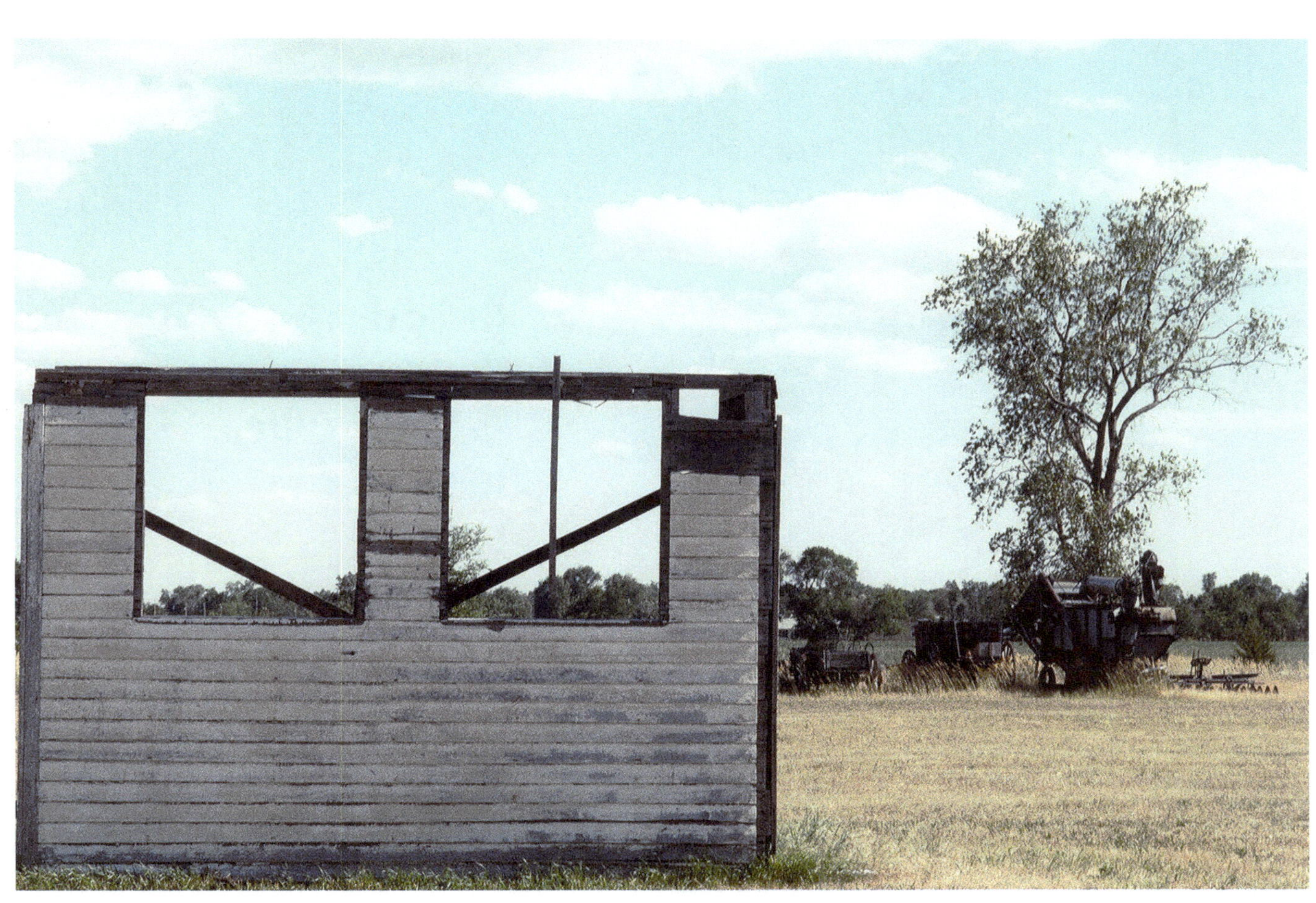

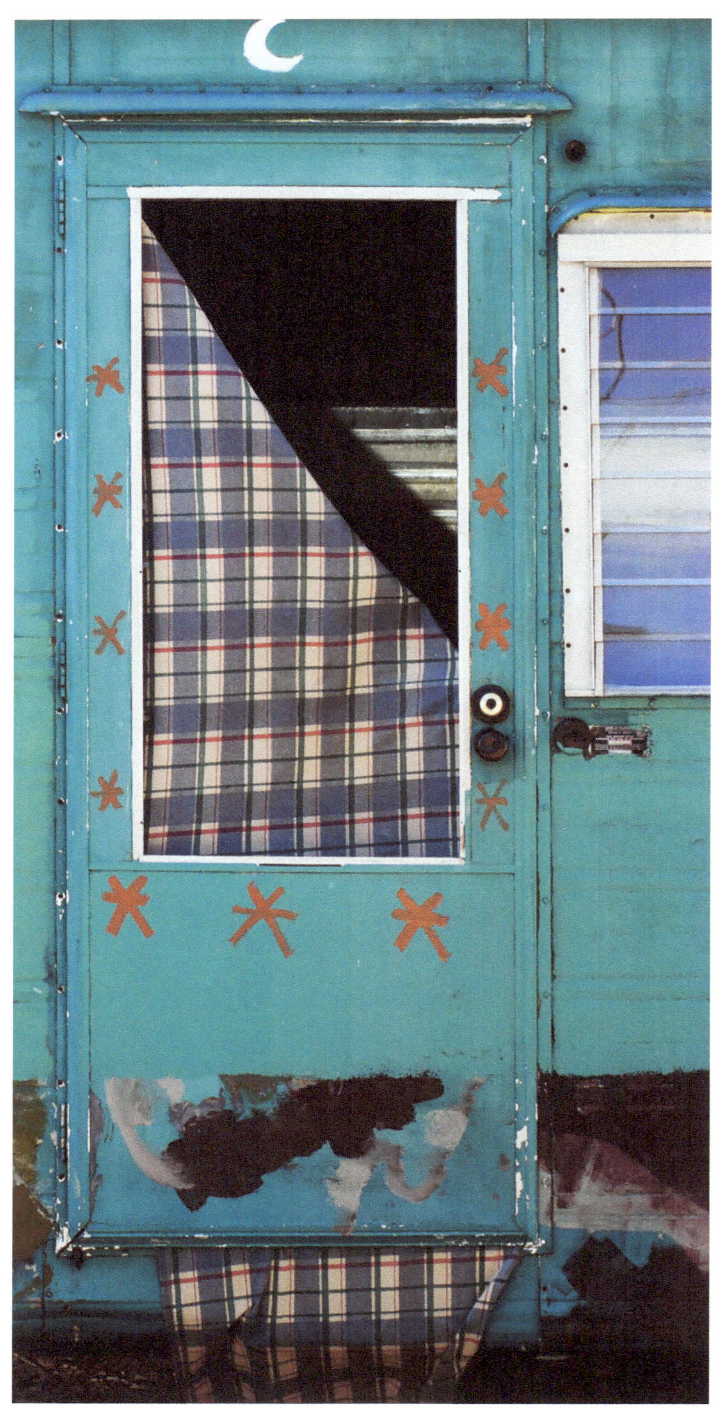

these days -
doors
are more often
meant
to keep
others from entering

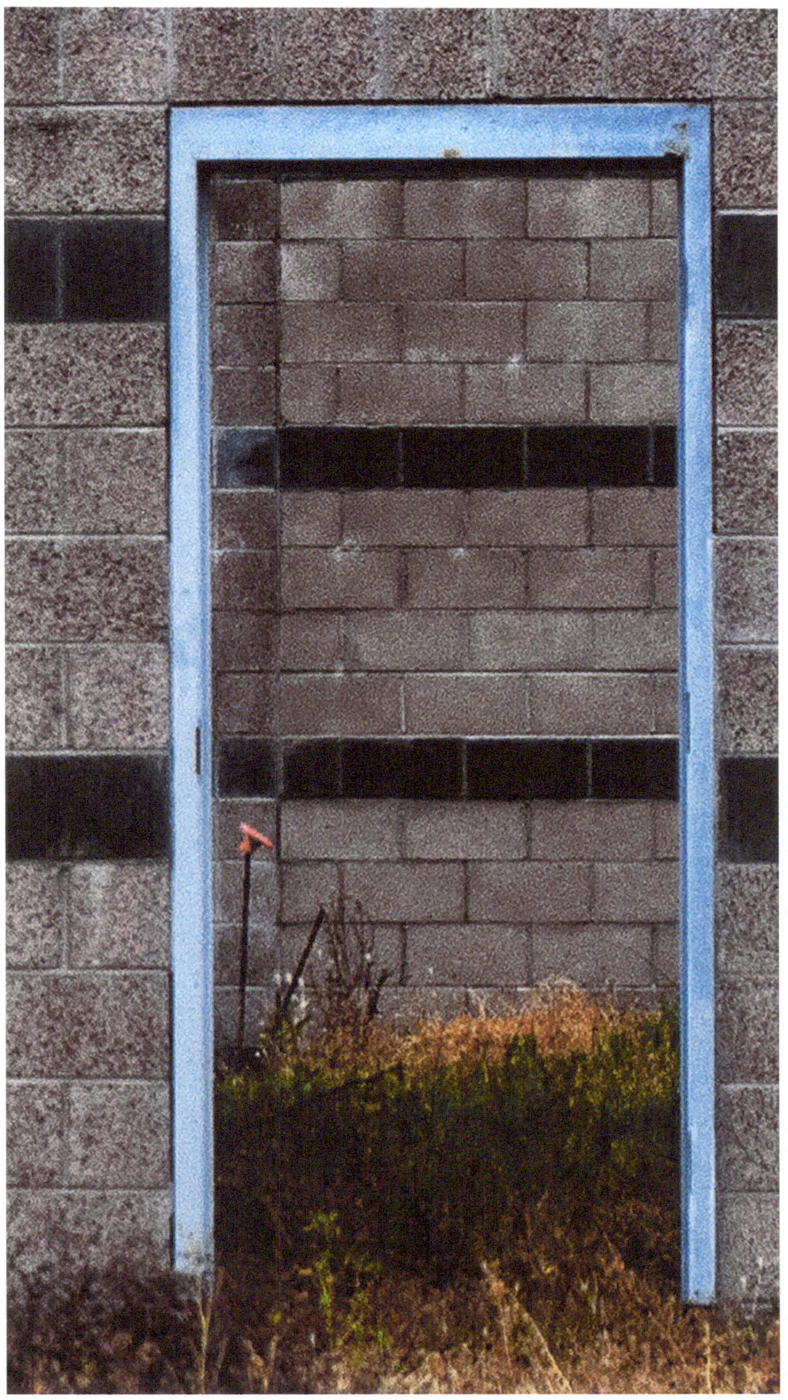

light
&
dark
flow freely
through windows

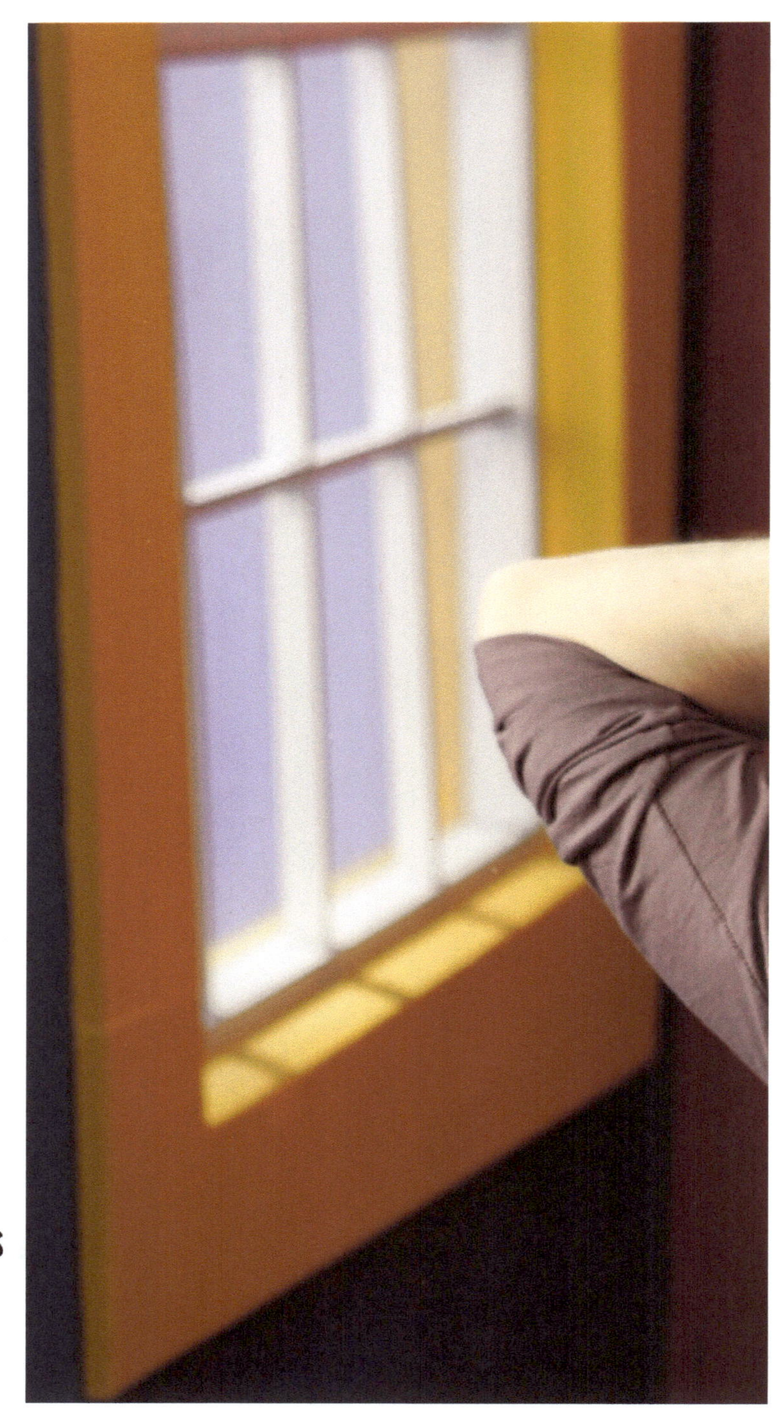

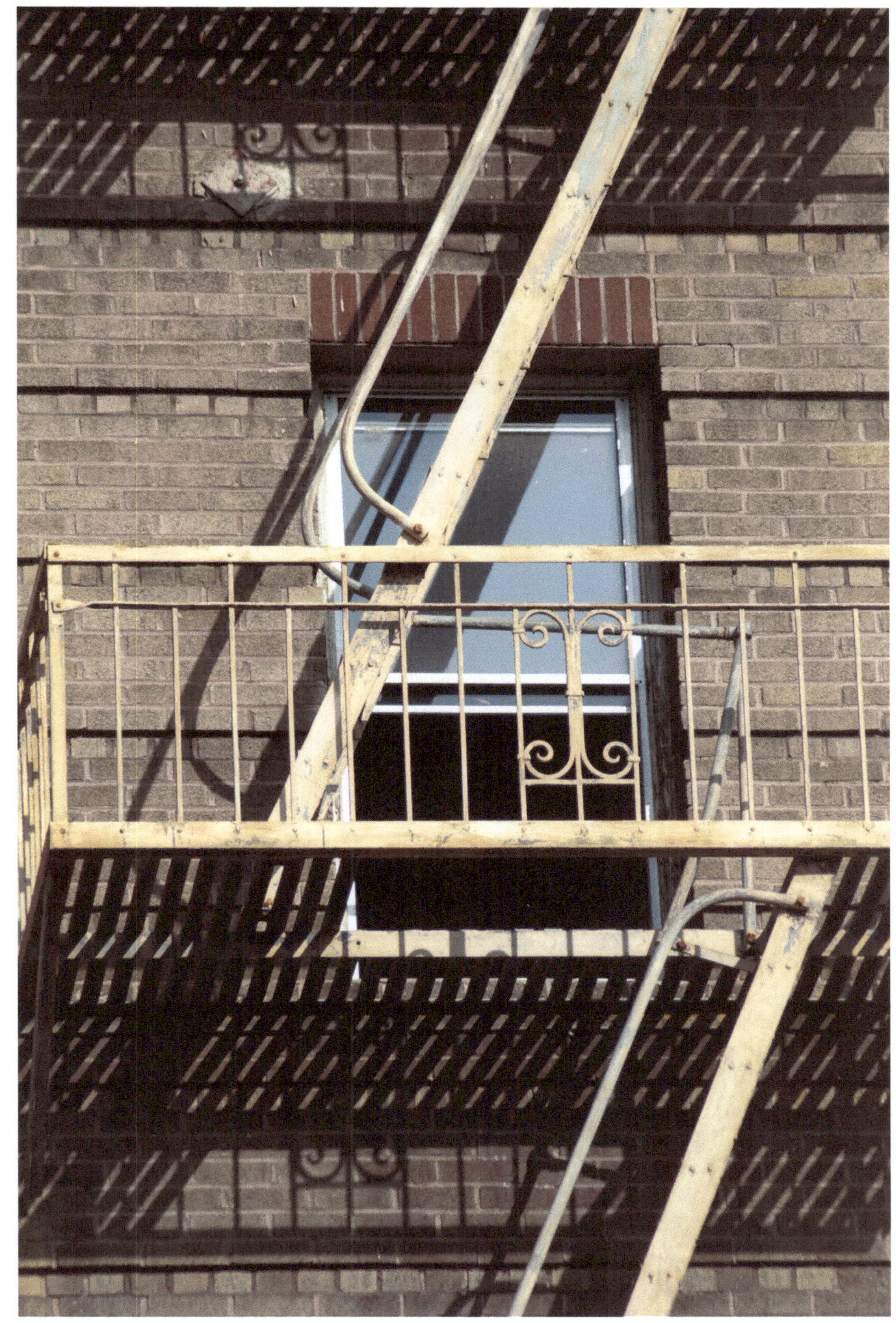

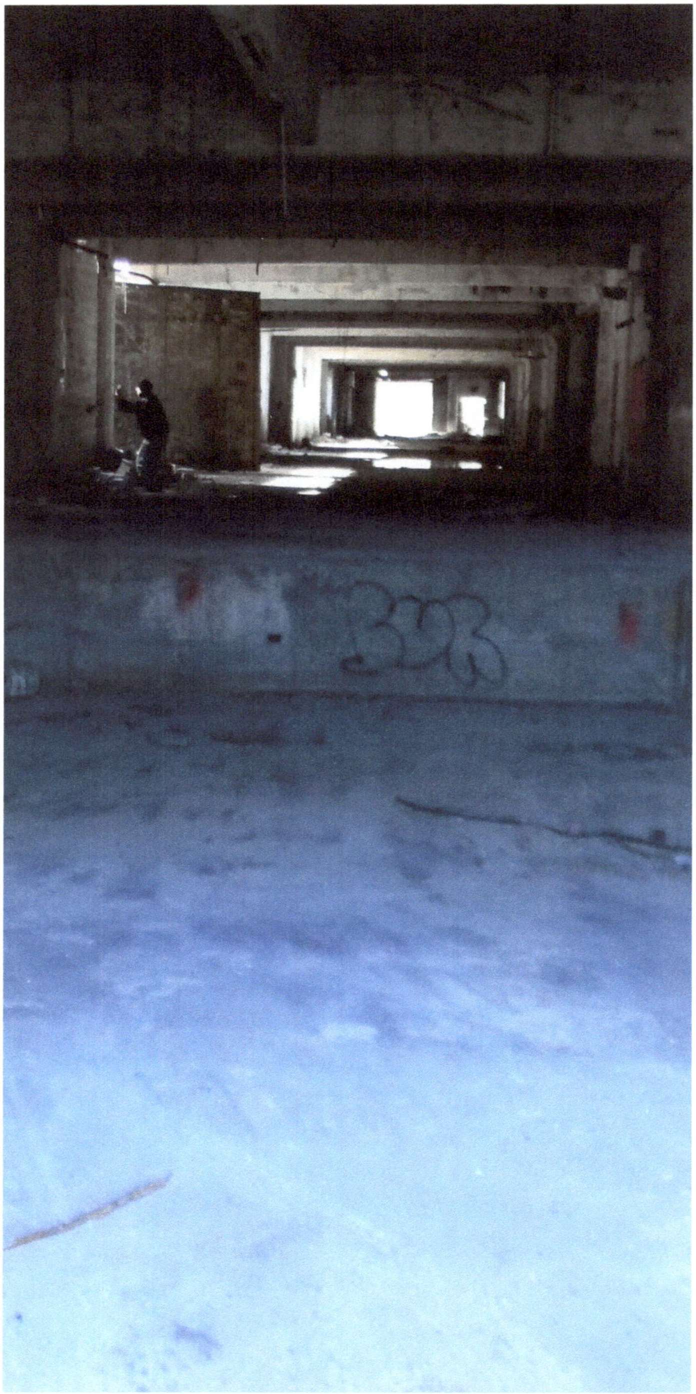

even with
no doors
no windows
there is
inside
& outside

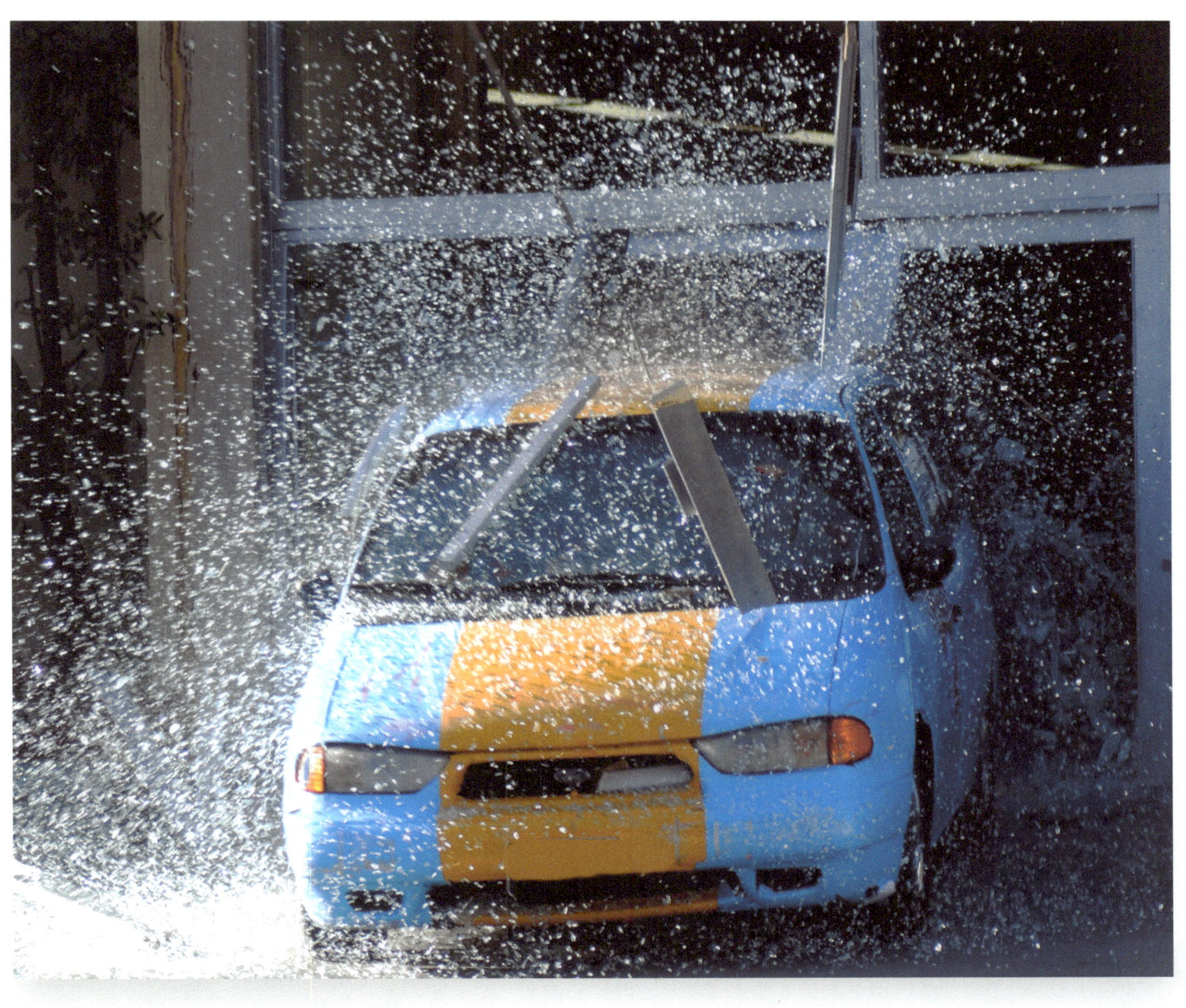

Some exits are more spectacular than others...

Windows & Doors
Imaginings

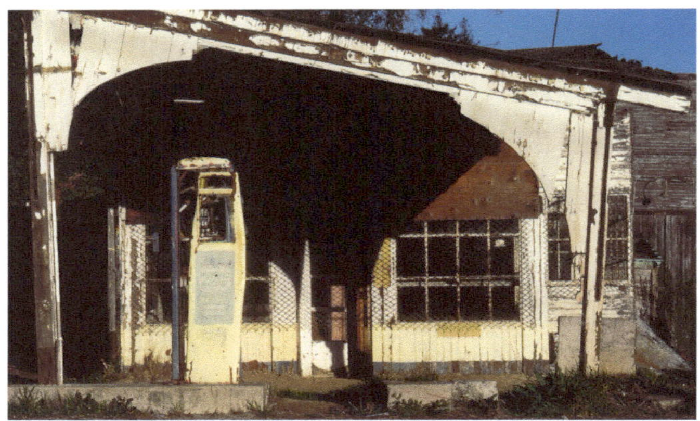

Interior and cover design by Allen Plone & Mark Anderson
All photographs and copy by Allen Plone

ISBN 978-1-954604-13-1

Published by Snow Lion Publishing, Los Angeles, CA

"Dedicated to the One I Love"

(Pauling & Bass, 1961 The Shirelles version,
the only one worth remembering.)

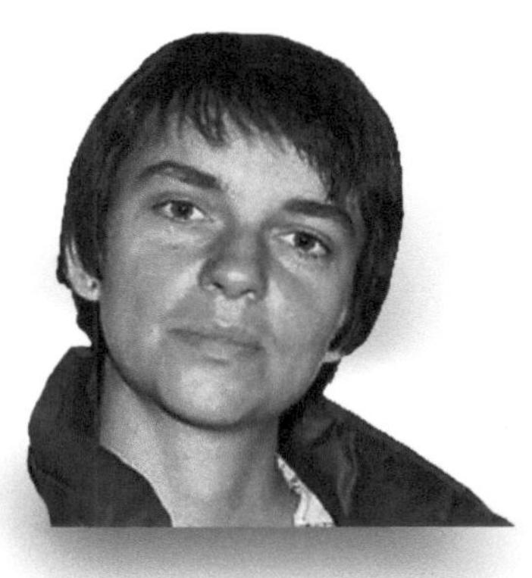

To my Carol, who opened every new window and door to my life.

www.ingramcontent.com/pod-product-compliance
Lightning Source LLC
LaVergne TN
LVHW071630100826
845154LV00007BA/120
9781954604131